Your truth is God's truth
and always your surest answer —
as awesome as the night sky,
as simple as a child's smile,
as loud as a pounding heartbeat,
and as quiet as a breath taken
in unity with Him.

— *"Conversations with God"*
as brought through by
Neale Donald Walsch

ON EARTH
as it is in
HEAVEN

Paintings by N.A. Noël
Story by N.A. Noël and John Wm. Sisson

My soul can find no staircase to Heaven unless it be through the Earth's loveliness.

– *Michelangelo*

This book is dedicated to
Georgia, who loved me, and
to all my friends and family.
It is on the wind from your wings that I fly...
and it is your light that guides me.

– N. A. Noël

With love and affection
to my brother Fred, who has been
my guardian angel all my life.

– John Wm. Sisson

Rosie stood there in Heaven and stretched out her wings,
so soft and so white, such marvelous things!

Now she could flip as she flew in the air –
maybe fly to the stars…why, fly anywhere!

Just as she thought this, an angel appeared.
"Oh my," said the angel, "it's just as I feared.

"Those wings that we gave you may be a bit wide.
We could pluck them or tuck them or trim up the side."

"Forgive me," said Rosie, "I don't know your name.
Please, may I keep them the way that they came?

"I like all this white and I like all this fluff.
I like all the things I can do with this stuff."

"Wisdom is my name. I'll be your good friend.
When little ones come here, I'm the angel they send.

"I'm glad that you're happy with Heaven's new gift.
They're wings for your spirit, to give you a lift!

"It always takes wisdom to see your way through,
especially up here, where all things seem new."

"You're right!" giggled Rosie. "Why, look over there!
Those crystals are gleaming and floating in air!"

"Rosie," said Wisdom, "remember the mirth
and laughter and fun when it snowed back on Earth?

"Those gentle flakes, like a lamb in the snow,
are glimpses of Heaven and the beauty we know.

"Like these flowers I'm wearing, entwined in my crown,
are proof to us all that God is around.

"Think back to the summer, when you walked by the sea,
with the waves full of sunlight…that sunlight was me!

"Like the seagull who waits for the wind to take flight,
we all have to choose what's wrong or what's right.

"You need to look and learn to take time
to see all God's beauty and, especially, be kind.

"These things are so easy, when you know God is here.
He's always beside you and within you, my dear.

"You are His child and always have been,
and so are your friends, both Rachel and Ben.

"Remember last fall with the leaves on the ground?
Remember the fawn the three of you found?

"You wondered at nature and how she revealed
the mystery and magic of what she concealed.

"This light of God's wisdom is something we share –
on Earth, as in Heaven…why, it's everywhere!"

"Oh please, precious Wisdom, may I go back to Earth,
to show Ben and Rachel what life's really worth?

"Rachel is two
and Ben is only three.
I know they may wonder,
when they think about me.

"How can I tell them I want them to know
that God's all around them, just like the young doe
whose sweetness is hidden as she lies in the leaves,
but is easily found by someone's good deeds?

"I'll touch their hearts, when a cloud passes by,
and whenever it's dark, I'll be their star in the sky.

"When flowers are blooming, I'll let them know
that Heaven is found in the roses that grow.

"I'll open their eyes to all they can see
and be to each other the best they can be."

"In a second you'll be there, and so will the dawn.
You can show them the seagull, the lamb, and the fawn.

"Go tell the children to tell all their friends
that love is forever and love never ends.

"Awaken the knowledge that shows them the worth
of knowing that Heaven can be here on Earth!"

Rosie looked toward the stars as she fluffed up her wings.
"I'll go back as an angel and show them these things."

"God will be pleased," said Wisdom, "by the good that you do,
which brings out the spirit of the love within you.

"He must have known, when He ordered your wings,
the size of your love and the gifts that it brings.

"Now soar as an angel through God's starry night,
and bring to your friends His wisdom and light."

This story is in memory of Therrian.